Trivia Math: A Problem a Day

Volume 1

Math Adventures in Science, Social Studies, Sports, and Entertainment

Carole Greenes
George Immerzeel
Marcie Abramson
Jeanette Caramagna
Suzanne Chapin
Christina Fritz
John Jordan
Sheri Katzman
Karen Tripoli
Susan Waiter

Creative
Publications
P.O. Box 10328   Palo Alto, CA 94303

Notes to the Teacher

Trivia Math: A Problem a Day, Volume 1 is a collection of problems and experiences that will challenge students to use mathematics to solve real-life problems. All events in this collection are true; the data are actual data. *Trivia Math* has been developed for use by students in regular classrooms in grades 5-8, and for gifted students in grade 4. There are four categories of problems: science, social studies, sports, and entertainment. Each category includes problems related to a variety of topics, such as the following:

Science:	botany, zoology, astronomy, physics, geometry, and other mathematical topics
Social studies:	world geography, history, economics, and government
Sports:	baseball, table tennis, polo, basketball, track and field, football, swimming, and Olympic Games
Entertainment:	theater, literature, music, art, motion pictures, and board and card games

To solve the problems, students must use previously learned mathematics as well as prior knowledge about the various topics.

For each of the 36 weeks of the school year, there are five daily problems and one poster problem. The daily problems are organized by category: Monday—science; Tuesday—entertainment; Wednesday—social studies; Thursday—sports. The Friday problem is selected from any of the four categories.

The poster problems are designed to challenge students' ingenuity in obtaining data and in problem solving. To solve the poster problems, students must conduct experiments and use reference materials such as maps, almanacs, and encyclopedias. They may have to acquire some data by consulting businesses and contacting public information services.

You may wish to duplicate the pages of daily problems for the students. You can give each student a whole page of problems at one time, or you can cut the problems apart and distribute them daily. Students can work individually or in pairs to solve the daily problems, and may complete them in class or as homework.

It is suggested that you place a copy of the week's poster problem on a bulletin board on Monday and then discuss the students' solutions with them on Friday. Because these problems are complex, it is recommended that students work in groups of two or more to solve the problems. Group problem-solving enhances communication, promotes hypothesis formation, and develops logical reasoning.

Solutions to all problems are given at the end of this book. For the poster problems, the data are presented as well as the answers. At times, students will find that their answers differ from the solutions given in the book, particularly for problems which require experimental data or information from reference materials. Historians and scientists are not always in agreement about certain facts, and as a result, sources often disagree on data.

© 1986 Creative Publications
P.O. Box 10328
Palo Alto, California 94303
Printed in U.S.A.
ISBN: 0-88488-343-4

1 2 3 4 5 6 7 8 9 10. 8 9 8 7 6

MONDAY

What is the greatest four-digit palindrome?

TUESDAY

In Monopoly™, what is the difference in price between the least expensive property and the most expensive property?

WEDNESDAY

The *Titanic* hit an iceberg at 11:59 P.M., April 15, 1912. The ship sank 7,260 seconds later. At what time did the *Titanic* sink?

THURSDAY

What is the area of the playing space inside a baseball diamond?

FRIDAY

The number of bones in a human foot is the same as the number of letters in the alphabet. How many foot bones are there in a group of 12 people?

POSTER PROBLEM

Cranberries are "dry picked" by mechanical harvesters that look like giant lawn mowers. The harvesters have rotating teeth that revolve through the vines and comb off the berries, which are then dropped into a box. A harvester machine can cover $1\frac{1}{2}$ acres and pick 10,000 pounds of fresh cranberries in a day. How many tons of cranberries can be harvested by 3 machines in 5 days?

MONDAY

Each year in the Chinese calendar is named after one of 12 animals. The year 1985 was the Year of the Ox. How many years in the 20th century are "Years of the Ox?"

TUESDAY

What's the greatest number of quarter notes possible in one bar of music in $\frac{4}{4}$ time?

WEDNESDAY

Cleopatra was 39 years old when she died in 30 B.C. In what year was Cleopatra born?

THURSDAY

How many more events are there in a decathlon than a triathlon?

FRIDAY

In the novel, *Robinson Crusoe*, Crusoe was stranded on an island for 10,280 days. To the nearest year, how many years was he stranded?

POSTER PROBLEM

A clock shows the correct time on May 1 at 1:00 P.M. The clock loses 20 minutes a day. What will be the next date when this clock shows the correct time?

MONDAY

The greatest common factor of 51 and 18 is the number of times John Glenn orbited the Earth. How many orbits did Glenn make?

TUESDAY

The first issue of a *Superman* comic book appeared on the newsstands in June, 1938. Then came *Batman*. The number of months between the two comic book debuts is the only two-digit palindromic prime. When did *Batman* appear on the newsstands?

WEDNESDAY

John Adams was the second U.S. President. He was elected to office in 1796 and served one term. Each of the next three presidents served two terms in office. The sixth U.S. President was John Adams' son, John Quincy Adams. In what year was John Quincy Adams elected President of the United States?

THURSDAY

A Ping-Pong ball weighs about $\frac{1}{10}$ of an ounce. How many Ping-Pong balls together weigh 1 pound?

FRIDAY

The famous comet Kohoutek is next due to appear in the year 76974. It last appeared 75 millenniums before the year 76974. When did Kohoutek last appear?

POSTER PROBLEM

How many steps would you have to take to walk from Los Angeles to San Francisco? (Decide on the length of an "average" step.)

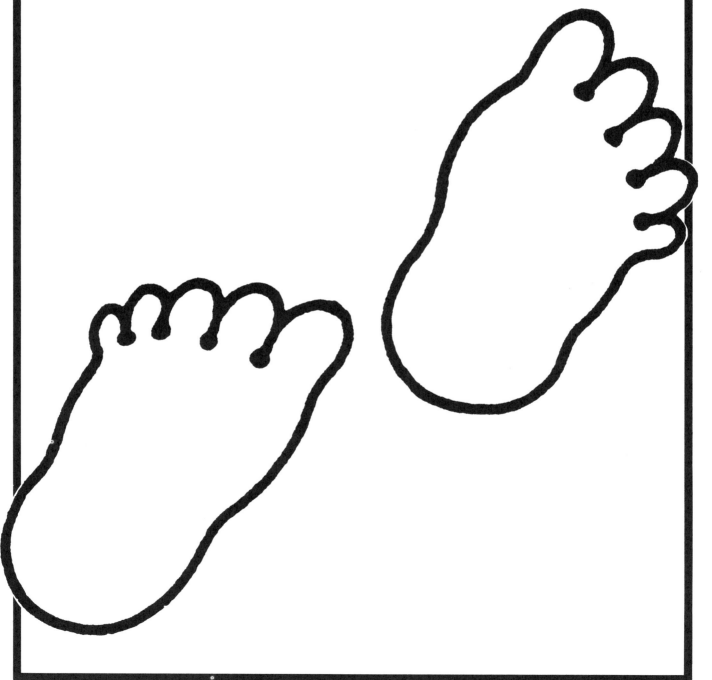

MONDAY

How many years is "four score and seven?"

TUESDAY

Katharine Hepburn has won the same number of Academy Awards as the number of prime numbers less than 10. How many Academy Awards has Hepburn won?

WEDNESDAY

How many years after the Declaration of Independence was George Washington inaugurated as the first President of the U.S.? The answer is a two-digit prime number. The ones' digit of the answer is 2 more than the tens' digit. The product of the digits is a prime number.

THURSDAY

The basketball player, Wilt Chamberlain, is 7 feet 1 inch tall. How many inches above his head is the rim of the basket when he is standing under the net?

FRIDAY

The diameter of a baseball is about 3 inches. How many baseballs placed side-by-side would it take to make a line of baseballs that would stretch from first base to home plate?

January 9 is an odd-number date. How many odd-number dates are there in a year that is not a leap year?

JANU

		1	2	3
7	8	⑨	10	
14	15	16	17	

MONDAY

The span of the Golden Gate Bridge in San Francisco Bay is 1080 feet less than a mile long. How many feet long is the span?

TUESDAY

In a game of tic-tac-toe, what is the greatest number of squares that may be left unmarked when the game is won?

WEDNESDAY

How many years before Geraldine Ferraro ran for Vice President did women receive the right to vote? The answer is the only two-digit number that is both a square and a cube!

THURSDAY

The number of rings on the Olympic flag is a prime number that is a factor of 105, 20, and 30. How many rings are there?

FRIDAY

The number of days that it takes Mercury to revolve around the sun is a palindromic number. Each digit is a cube greater than 1. How many days does it take Mercury to revolve around the sun?

POSTER PROBLEM

Two out of every three people in the United States wear eyeglasses. About how many people in the United States wear eyeglasses?

MONDAY

A sperm whale has been recorded at a depth of 620 fathoms. How many feet is this record depth?

TUESDAY

The longest disco-dancing marathon began on January 18, 1982, and was 371 hours long. If the dancing began at 9 A.M. on January 18, on what date did the marathon end?

WEDNESDAY

How many more stars are on the United States flag today than on the flag created by Betsy Ross in 1777?

THURSDAY

The number of times that the Chicago Cubs have won the World Series is a multiple of every number. How many times have the Cubs won the World Series?

FRIDAY

A recorder is a type of flute. The number of holes on a recorder is the only prime factor of 28. How many holes are on a recorder?

On a trip to Washington, D.C. you visit the Washington Monument. You take the elevator up to the top of the monument. You're feeling very ambitious, so you decide to walk down. At the rate of two steps per second, how many minutes and seconds will it take you to walk down?

MONDAY

What is the sum of the number of corners, the number of sides, and the number of edges on a cube?

TUESDAY

The largest painting now in existence is the *Battle of Gettysburg*. The painting weighs 1,792 pounds more than 5 tons. How many pounds does the painting weigh?

WEDNESDAY

When John Hancock signed the Declaration of Independence, his age was a multiple of 13 and the sum of the digits was twelve. How old was Hancock?

THURSDAY

The diameter of a tennis ball is $2\frac{1}{2}$ inches. How many tennis balls will fit in a can $2\frac{1}{2}$ inches in diameter and a foot long?

FRIDAY

In what year will the United States celebrate its tercentennial birthday?

How many N.F.L. footballs laid end-to-end would reach from goal line to goal line on a football field?

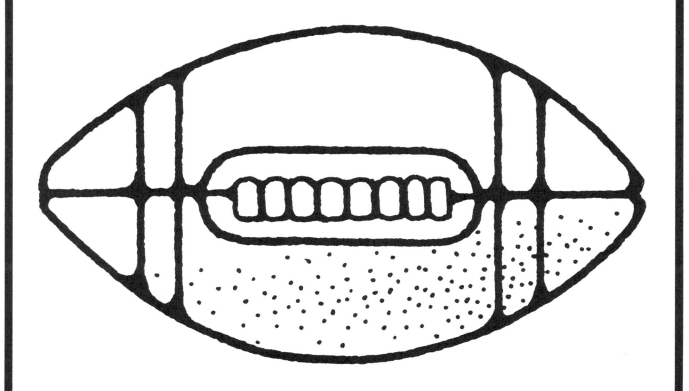

MONDAY

How many computers are in the room if all but two are made by Apple, all but two are made by IBM, and all but two are made by Commodore?

TUESDAY

J. S. Bach had the top-selling classical album in 1983, and Michael Jackson had the top-selling pop album. Bach was born long before 1958, the year of Jackson's birth. When was Bach born? The number of years separating the dates of birth is a three-digit number. Each digit is a prime number; the tens' digit the largest, the hundreds' digit the smallest. The sum of the digits is 12 and the product of the digits is 42.

WEDNESDAY

Plastic credit cards were first issued in the U.S. 10 years before Kennedy took office as President. In what year were plastic credit cards first issued? The sum of the digits of the year is 15 and the product of the digits is 45.

THURSDAY

What fraction of the pins are in the back row in bowling?

FRIDAY

In gymnastics the rings are suspended from a bar that is 17 feet 11 inches from the floor. Ropes hold the rings 9 feet 9 inches below the bar. How far are the tops of the rings from the floor?

POSTER PROBLEM

The silent film, *The Gold Rush*, is made up of 69,120 individual pictures or frames that are projected on the screen. The silent film, *The Kid*, is made up of 49,920 frames. How many minutes longer is *The Gold Rush* than *The Kid*? (Hint: In silent films, 16 frames a second were projected on a screen.)

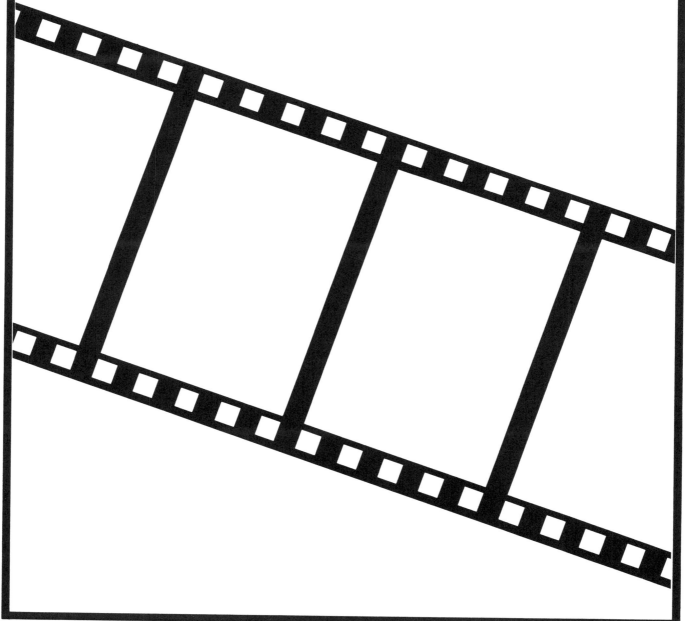

MONDAY

A number is balanced if exactly one digit is the sum of all the other digits. What is the greatest three-digit balanced number?

TUESDAY

The Sound of Music, one of the all-time favorite movies, won an Academy Award in what year? The sum of the digits of the year is 21 and the product of the digits is 270.

WEDNESDAY

The number of Supreme Court Justices is the greatest common factor of 18 and 27. How many Supreme Court Justices are there?

THURSDAY

How many laps must a person run around a quarter-mile track to run $9\frac{1}{2}$ miles?

FRIDAY

If a regular octahedron has a surface area of 32 square inches, what is the surface area of each face?

POSTER PROBLEM

Khufu built the largest Egyptian pyramid in 2580 B.C. The pyramid had 2.3 million stone blocks, each weighing 2.5 tons. The Great Wall of China, started in 246 B.C., contained enough rock to construct 120 pyramids the size of Khufu's pyramid. How many pounds of rock were in the Great Wall of China when it was built?

MONDAY

One of the lightest creatures is a bee hummingbird. Eighteen bee hummingbirds together weigh one pound. How many bee hummingbirds together weigh one kilogram?

TUESDAY

At the beginning of a game of checkers, what fraction of the squares are not covered by checker pieces?

WEDNESDAY

In 79 A.D. Mount Vesuvius erupted and covered the cities of Herculaneum and Pompeii with volcanic ash and mud. Serious work on uncovering Herculaneum didn't begin until the 20th century. In what year did excavation of Herculaneum begin? The sum of the year's digits is 19. The product of the digits is 126. The tens' digit is less than the ones' digit.

THURSDAY

Babe Ruth called his famous baseball bat, Black Betsy. How many ounces did this bat weigh? The answer is a two-digit palindrome. The product of the digits is 2^4.

FRIDAY

In music, how many notes are in $4\frac{1}{2}$ octaves?

POSTER PROBLEM

How much longer would it take to run the marathon at a speed of one mile in 5.5 minutes than one mile in 5 minutes?

MONDAY

How many more corners does a stop sign have than a yield sign?

TUESDAY

In a survey it was found that, on an average, each person watched 30 hours and 47 minutes of television per week. How much television would each person have watched in a year?

WEDNESDAY

It is 963 miles from Boston to Chicago by highway. If a bicycle rider set out on January 24, and averaged 50 miles per day, when would the cyclist arrive in Chicago?

THURSDAY

In a single elimination Ping-Pong tournament with 20 players, how many games must be played to determine a winner?

FRIDAY

The parking meter was invented by Carl C. Magee in the first half of the 20th century. In what year was it first used? The digits of the year sum to 18 and the year is divisible by 5.

POSTER PROBLEM

If each of the U.S. Supreme Court Justices shook hands with each of the other Justices, once and only once, how many handshakes would take place?

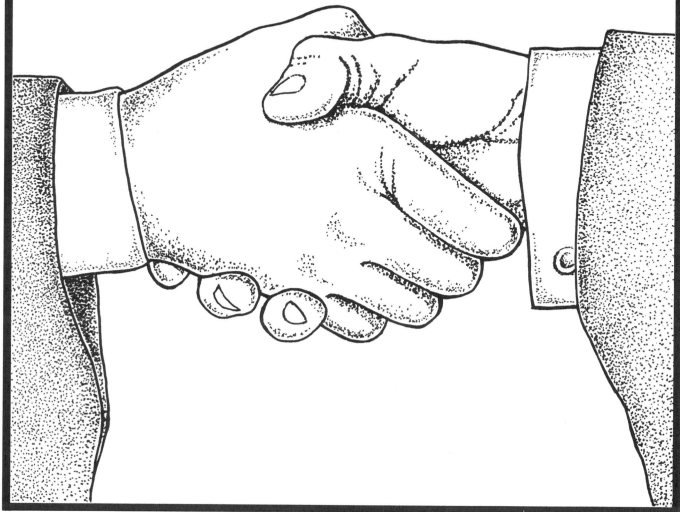

MONDAY

What time is it on a twelve-hour clock $6\frac{1}{2}$ hours after a military clock shows 1500?

TUESDAY

In what year was Bruce Springsteen born? Two digits in the year are the same. The sum of the digits is a prime and the product of the digits is the square of 18.

WEDNESDAY

Berlin, prewar capital of Germany, lies within the borders of East Germany. The city is divided into East Berlin, with an area of 156 square miles and a population of 1,146,000; and West Berlin, with an area of 184 square miles and a population of 1,890,300. Which part of the city has more people per square mile and by how much?

THURSDAY

As of 1984, the New York Yankees had been in 33 World Series. They had won twice as many Series as they had lost. How many World Series had they won?

FRIDAY

The first Olympic marathon in 1896 was won by Greece in 2 hours, 58 minutes, 50 seconds. In 1984 Portugal won the marathon with a time of 2 hours, 9 minutes, 55 seconds. How much time did Portugal cut off the 1896 record?

POSTER PROBLEM

How many birthdays will you have celebrated when you are one million minutes old?

MONDAY

The thighbone or femur is the longest bone in the body. About $\frac{1}{4}$ of a person's height is the length of the femur. If a person's femur measures 18 inches, about how many feet tall is the person?

TUESDAY

Over a period of 38 years, beginning in 1884, Sara Winchester built a strange mystery house in San Jose, California. The house, at a cost of $5.5 million, eventually had 158 rooms and 40 stairways, some ending in midair. What was the avarage cost of each room in the house?

WEDNESDAY

How many years after the Pilgrims landed at Plymouth Rock was gold discovered in California?

THURSDAY

What is the distance in feet from the foul line to the head pin of a bowling lane, if $\frac{1}{3}$ of the distance is 240 inches?

FRIDAY

How many years will it take to spend one million dollars if you spend one hundred dollars each day?

POSTER PROBLEM

Imagine a highway from the Earth to the Moon. If you left Earth on January 1, 1990, and drove at an average speed of 55 miles per hour, day and night, on what day would you arrive on the Moon?

MONDAY

An adult opossum has 18 more teeth than an adult human. How many teeth does an adult opossum have? The sum of the digits of this number is 5 and the product of the digits is 0.

TUESDAY

How many "strings" are there on the instruments in a string quintet with two violins, two violas, and one cello?

WEDNESDAY

The people of New York City celebrated the centennial of the Brooklyn Bridge in 1983. When was the Brooklyn Bridge built?

THURSDAY

In horseshoe pitching, the two stakes are 40 feet apart. The horseshoe court itself is 46 feet long. Each stake is the same distance from the end of the court. How far is each stake from the end of the court?

FRIDAY

The first national broadcast of the television program "Sesame Street" was 51 days before New Year's Day in 1970. Give the date and the year of the "Sesame Street" premiere.

POSTER PROBLEM

The area of the checkerboard is 144 square inches. What is the length of a side of a small square on the checkerboard?

MONDAY

The maximum speed of a zebra is 40 miles per hour. At this speed, how long would it take the zebra to run one mile?

TUESDAY

Elvis Presley made 90 more "singles" than "albums" that were major hits. The total number of singles and albums is 250. How many singles hits did Presley make?

WEDNESDAY

What percent of the states in the U.S. do not border any other states?

THURSDAY

How many games are played in a 5 team round-robin tournament?

FRIDAY

In what year of the 18th century was Washington, D.C. selected as the United States capital? The year is a multiple of 10. The tens' digit is 2 more than the hundreds' digit.

How much more money is a pound of tennis shoes than a pound of a Chevrolet 4-door sedan?

MONDAY

In the sequence ABCDEABCDE ... what is the 63rd letter?

TUESDAY

How many different 2- by 2-squares are on a chessboard?

WEDNESDAY

Seat belts were first used in cars 19 years before the first moon walk. In what year were seat belts first used in cars?

THURSDAY

A chukker in polo is a period of play that is $7\frac{1}{2}$ minutes long. There are 8 chukkers in a game of polo. How many chukkers are left in the game after 45 minutes of play?

FRIDAY

Pete Rose set a new record in 1985 for total number of hits in his career. He set this new record on the anniversary of the previous record-holder Ty Cobb's last time at-bat. In what year was Ty Cobb last at-bat? The number of years between records is a two-digit number. Both digits are primes. The smallest prime is the tens' digit. The sum of the digits is 12.

POSTER PROBLEM

The fastest elevator in the Empire State Building moves at an average rate of 20 feet per second. To the nearest second, how long would it take the elevator to travel from the observation deck on the 69th floor to the one on the 102nd floor? (Hint: There are 12 feet between floors.)

MONDAY

The fastest temperature change on record occurred in South Dakota. On January 22, 1943, at 7:30 A.M., the temperature was -2° Fahrenheit. In two minutes the temperature increased by 40°. What was the temperature at 7:32 A.M.?

TUESDAY

Beethoven composed 4 more symphonies than piano concertos. How many piano concertos did Beethoven compose?

WEDNESDAY

The number of times the word "one" appears on a U.S. dollar bill is the same as the number that is the smallest one-digit even cube. How many times does the word "one" appear on a dollar bill?

THURSDAY

The Indianapolis-500 is a 500-mile automobile race with each lap $2\frac{1}{2}$ miles long. How many laps does a winner complete to win the race?

FRIDAY

Gravity on the moon is $\frac{1}{6}$ of the earth's gravity. If a person weighs 180 pounds on earth, how much less would that person weigh on the moon?

POSTER PROBLEM

What is the total number of dots on all the dominoes in a regular set of dominoes?

MONDAY

Days are shorter on Jupiter than on Earth. A Jupiter day is 14 hours 10 minutes shorter than an Earth day. How long is a day on Jupiter?

TUESDAY

In what year of the 19th century was Sir Arthur Conan Doyle's first novel about Detective Sherlock Holmes published? The tens' and hundreds' digits are identical cubes. The sum of the digits is 24 and the product of the digits is 448.

WEDNESDAY

How many states and their state capitals begin with the same letter?

THURSDAY

How much greater is the length of a football field (from goal line to goal line) than its width?

FRIDAY

When was the yo-yo first produced? The ones' digit and the hundreds' digit of the year are identical squares and divisible by three. The tens' digit is the only even prime number.

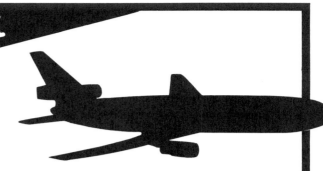

POSTER PROBLEM

How much longer would it take a car, traveling at an average speed of 42 miles per hour, to make the trip from San Francisco to New York, than a DC10 jet flying at an average speed of 500 miles per hour?

MONDAY

One of the largest prehistoric creatures, a type of pterosaur, had a wingspan of at least 36 feet. The smallest airplane, the *Stits Skybaby*, has a wingspan of 7 feet 2 inches. What percent of the prehistoric creature's wingspan is the *Skybaby*'s wingspan?

TUESDAY

E.T. is one of the all-time top-grossing films, at $209.6 million. *Gone With the Wind*, filmed in 1939, is in the top 15; grossing 36.6 percent of *E.T.*'s total. How much has *Gone With the Wind* made?

WEDNESDAY

The Verrazano-Narrows bridge in New York is the longest suspension bridge in North America. If you were traveling across the bridge, a distance of 4,260 feet, at a speed of 55 miles per hour, how long would it take you to cross the bridge?

THURSDAY

How many 10-yard markers are there between goal lines on a football field?

FRIDAY

The longest frontier between countries is between the U.S. and Canada, a distance of 3,987 miles. How many weeks would it take someone, jogging at an average speed of 10 minutes per mile for 8 hours a day, to jog the length of this frontier?

POSTER PROBLEM

What is the value of 16 metric tons of nickels?

MONDAY

The part of an iceberg which is below water is about seven times the size of the part above water. What fraction of the iceberg is above water?

TUESDAY

The number of holes on the largest harmonica in the world is 6 less than 30 dozen. How many holes are there on the largest harmonica?

WEDNESDAY

The shortest surface distance from Washington, D.C., to San Francisco is 2,442 miles. By car the distance is 2,864 miles. What percent of the distance by car is extra, due to man and nature?

THURSDAY

In 1962, Wilt Chamberlain set the record for the greatest number of points scored by a player in one game. He made 28 free throws and 36 field goals. How many points did Chamberlain score in that game?

FRIDAY

The longest recorded punt in football was made by Steve O'Neil of the New York Jets on September 21, 1969. The length of the punt was 6 feet less than the length of the field from goal line to goal line. How many yards long was O'Neil's punt?

POSTER PROBLEM

The Richter Scale is used to measure the strength of earthquakes. How many times stronger is an earthquake measuring 8 than an earthquake measuring 2 on the Richter Scale?

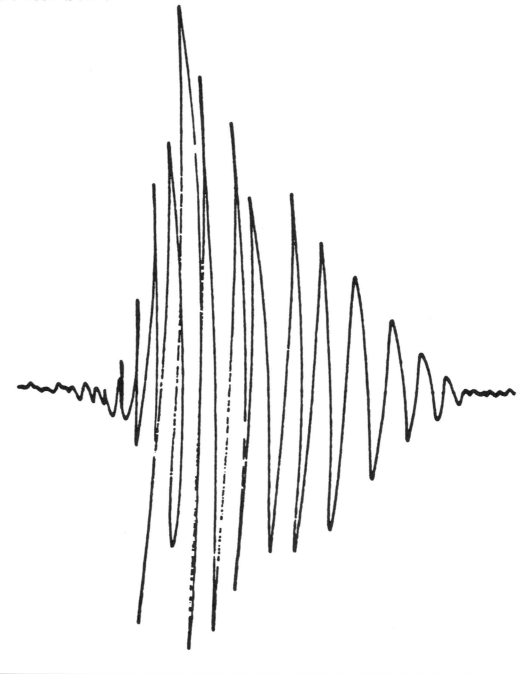

MONDAY

How many degrees are between northeast and southeast on a compass?

TUESDAY

With a regular deck of playing cards, how many different 5-card hands with 4 queens are possible?

WEDNESDAY

The United States flag has either 5 or 6 stars in each row. How many rows with 5 stars are on the flag?

THURSDAY

Five college football players share the record for the longest pass. How many yards is the record pass? The answer is a palindromic number. Each digit is a square.

FRIDAY

In March, 1942, 107 inches of rainfall was recorded in Kukui, Hawaii. What was the average rainfall per hour for that month?

A toy boat is put into the Mississippi River at Itasca, Minnesota and travels downstream at an average speed of 3 miles per hour. How many days will it take the boat to reach the Gulf of Mexico?

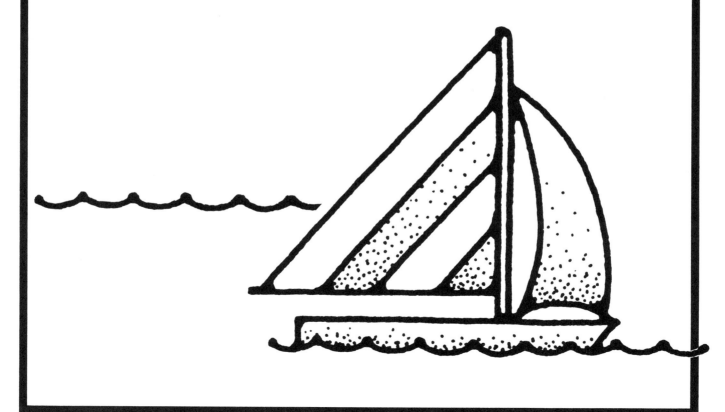

MONDAY

How many fortnights are there in $6\frac{1}{2}$ years?

TUESDAY

In what year of the 19th century was *Pinocchio* written? The sum of the digits in the year is 20 and the difference between the ones' and thousands' digits is 2.

WEDNESDAY

The number of electoral votes for a state is equal to the total number of U.S. Senators and Representatives from that state. New York has 41 electoral votes. How many Representatives does New York have?

THURSDAY

The boxing ring is a square with a maximum perimeter of 80 feet. What is the area of a boxing ring with the maximum perimeter?

FRIDAY

What is the sum of the numbers on the buttons of a push-button telephone?

POSTER PROBLEM

In *The Arabian Nights*, Scheherazade entertained the Sultan for one thousand one nights by telling a different story each night. If she had started on January 1, 1885, on what date would she have told the last story?

MONDAY

At a penny a digit, how much money would you earn for writing the counting numbers from 1 through 100?

TUESDAY

In 1976, the actor George Burns became an octogenarian. In what year was Burns born?

WEDNESDAY

New York is one of the most densely populated states and North Dakota one of the least populated. Based on the 1980 census, the population of New York State was 17,558,072, and the land area of the state is 47,377 square miles. North Dakota has a population of 652,717 with a land area of 70,665 square miles. In 1980, how many more people are there per square mile in New York than in North Dakota?

THURSDAY

How many times does a speed skater need to go around a 400-meter track to complete a 2-kilometer race?

FRIDAY

Alexander Graham Bell invented the telephone 100 years after the Declaration of Independence was signed. Samuel Morse invented Morse Code 24 years before Bell invented the phone. When did Morse invent Morse Code?

POSTER PROBLEM

How many dollar bills laid end-to-end form a line
one mile long?

MONDAY

On May 5, 1961, Alan B. Shepard became the first American in space. Two hundred ninety-one days later John Glenn became the first American to orbit the Earth. When did Glenn orbit the Earth?

TUESDAY

A bagpipe has the same number of pipes as the number of factors of 16. How many pipes are there?

WEDNESDAY

The Statue of Liberty and its pedestal are 302 feet tall. The statue is 2 feet taller than the pedestal. How many feet tall is the statue?

THURSDAY

A polo field is 300 yards long and 160 yards wide. A football field is 100 yards long and 160 feet wide. How many football fields would it take to cover a polo field?

FRIDAY

A softball weighs $\frac{2}{5}$ more than a baseball. A baseball and a softball together weigh 12 ounces. How much does a softball weigh?

POSTER PROBLEM

On a digital clock, some of the digits are displayed more often than others. In a 12-hour period of time, how many more minutes is at least one "1" displayed than at least one "9"?

MONDAY

The United States Department of Agriculture reports that each American eats an average of 176.4 pounds of meat a year. About how many ounces per day does each person eat?

TUESDAY

If you subscribe to a bimonthly magazine, how many issues of the magazine do you get in 2 years?

WEDNESDAY

What will be the date, including the year, of the first day in the 23rd century?

THURSDAY

Mary Decker has run an indoor mile in 4 minutes and 17.6 seconds. What was her average speed in miles per hour in that run?

FRIDAY

At the annual Calaveras County Jumping Frog contest, the frog "Ex Lax" jumped $210\frac{3}{4}$ inches. Robert Beamon set a long jump world record in 1968, jumping 29 feet $2\frac{1}{2}$ inches. How many inches longer than Ex Lax's jump was Beamon's jump?

POSTER PROBLEM

How many turns would a tennis ball make if it were rolled from one end of a tennis court to the other?

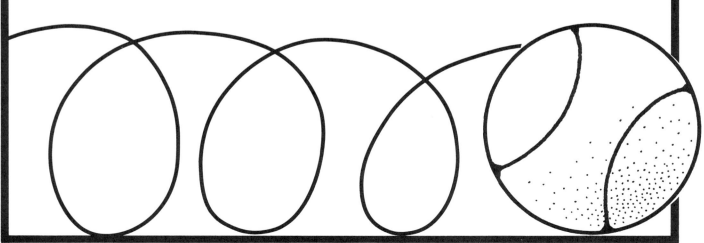

MONDAY

What is the Roman Numeral for 444?

TUESDAY

What is the total number of dots on a regular die?

WEDNESDAY

Franklin Delano Roosevelt had 5 times as many sons as daughters. He had 6 children altogether. How many daughters did he have?

THURSDAY

Hank Aaron made 755 homeruns. Babe Ruth made 41 fewer homeruns than Aaron. How many homeruns did Babe Ruth make in his baseball career?

FRIDAY

Bobby Fischer was the first American to win the World Chess championship. When he won his first U.S. championship, his age was one less than the number of black pieces on a chess board at the start of a game. How old was Fischer when he won his first U.S. championship?

POSTER PROBLEM

If the Pilgrim ship, the *Mayflower*, could race the luxury ocean liner, the *QE2*, from England to the United States, how many days would the *QE2* wait for the *Mayflower*?

MONDAY

In what year was the element oxygen first identified? The year was 3 years after the only year in the 18th century that is a palindromic number.

TUESDAY

How many more white than black keys are on a piano?

WEDNESDAY

The Hundred Years War was fought between England and France from 1337 to 1453. How many years longer than a century was the war?

THURSDAY

What is the weight of the bowling ball that weighs 3 pounds plus $\frac{3}{4}$ of its weight?

FRIDAY

New York City was the first city in America whose population reached a million. This occured in the 19th century, 15 years after the Civil War. In what year did New York City's population reach one million?

When you hear the word "cords," you may think of corduroy slacks. But "cord" is also a unit of measure. Firewood is measured in cords. How many cords is 320 cubic feet of wood?

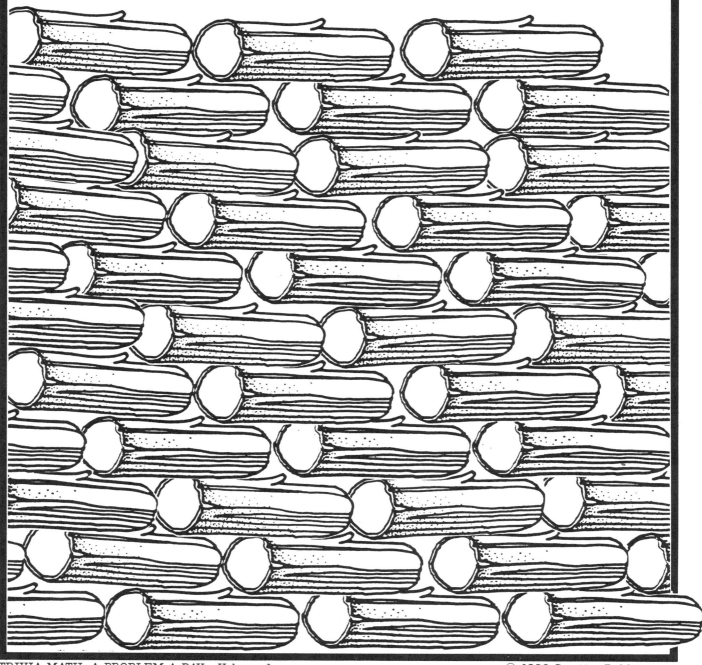

MONDAY

What is the total value of 13 rolls of quarters?

TUESDAY

The greatest common factor of 25 and 12 is the number of Academy Awards won by John Wayne. How many Academy Awards did he win?

WEDNESDAY

Henry Ford was born in 1863. He produced the Model T Ford during the first quarter of the 20th century. The sum of the digits of the year is 18. One of the digits is a zero. When did Ford produce the Model T?

THURSDAY

In the 1980 Winter Olympics, the U.S. won two bronze medals; twice as many silver medals as bronze; and three times as many gold medals as bronze. How many medals did the U.S. win?

FRIDAY

If the balls in a game of pool are lined up, from the smallest numbered ball to the largest numbered ball, which ball would be in the middle?

POSTER PROBLEM

Five cards are picked from a deck of cards:

- The cards are cards with numbers.
- Each card has a different number.
- Every suit is represented.
- The sum of the numbers on the even-numbered cards is equal to the sum of the numbers on the odd-numbered cards.
- The sum of the numbers on the black cards is 22.
- The sum of the numbers on the red cards is 10.
- The sum of the spades is 16.
- The lowest-numbered card is a heart.

What are the cards?

MONDAY

In the binary number system, 1100011 is the name for the largest two-digit palindrome in base ten. What base ten number does this binary number represent?

TUESDAY

According to surveys, the television program with the largest audience to date was the "M*A*S*H" special in 1983. It is reported that 59 percent of the 85 million television households were tuned in. How many households saw this program?

WEDNESDAY

The height of the Horseshoe Falls in Niagra Falls, Canada, is 4 feet more than 132 feet. What is the height of the Horseshoe Falls?

THURSDAY

In Little League baseball, how many feet farther do you need to run for a triple than a single?

FRIDAY

If you get four sticks of butter to a pound, and each stick of butter is $\frac{1}{2}$ cup, how many cups of butter is a pound of butter?

POSTER PROBLEM

What are the dimensions of the cube that is made from 1,000,000 sugar cubes?

MONDAY

How many bills with Lincoln's picture are equal in value to a bill with Jackson's picture?

TUESDAY

How many gifts were given in *The Twelve Days of Christmas*?

WEDNESDAY

The second longest river in the world is the Amazon, in South America, and it is approximately 3,912 miles long. If you traveled an average speed of 20 knots for 24 hours a day, how long would it take you to travel the length of the Amazon?

THURSDAY

Jim Brown of the Cleveland Browns holds the record for the most career touchdowns with 126. He made 86 more touchdowns by running than by receiving. How many touchdowns did Jim Brown make by receiving?

FRIDAY

Lucille Ball was 40 years old when the show "I Love Lucy" premiered. Lucille Ball was born in the year whose thousands', tens', and ones' digits are the same. In what year did "I Love Lucy" premiere?

POSTER PROBLEM

Find the country that is best described by the following facts:

- The capital is located at 35° 40′ N. latitude.
- The elevation of the capital is 30 feet.
- The area of the country is approximately 144,000 square miles and the population is about 120,000,000.

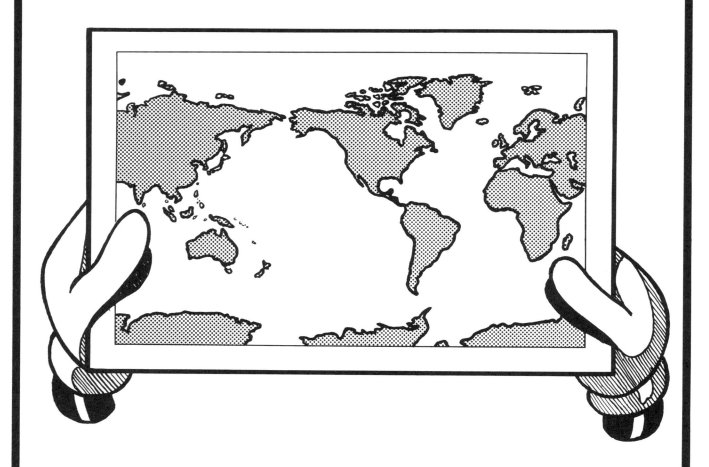

MONDAY

In England weight is measured in stone. A man who weighs 10 stone weighs 140 pounds. An African elephant, weighing 7 tons, weighs how many stone?

TUESDAY

At the age of 5, Wolfgang Amadeus Mozart composed "Twinkle Twinkle Little Star." Thirty years later in 1791 Mozart composed the opera, *The Magic Flute*. In what year was Mozart born?

WEDNESDAY

Pablo Picasso, the famous painter, was born on October 25 in the only year in the nineteenth century that is a palindrome. In what year was Picasso born?

THURSDAY

What fraction of the baseball game is over when the fans take a traditional stretch?

FRIDAY

Shirley Chisholm was the first black U.S. Congresswoman. She represented New York City from 1969-1983. How many terms did she serve?

POSTER PROBLEM

If each person in the United States gave you a penny, and you laid the pennies end-to-end, how many miles long would the penny line be?

MONDAY

There are 25 sheets of paper in a quire. How many quires of paper are there in a ream?

TUESDAY

What percent of the property cards in Monopoly™ are Railroads?

WEDNESDAY

How many more states today must vote for a new amendment to the U.S. Constitution to be ratified than in 1940?

THURSDAY

The surface area of the table in table tennis is 45 square feet. The difference between the length and width is 4 feet. What is the length of the table?

FRIDAY

In the Olympic 400-meter hurdles, there is a distance of 45 meters before the first hurdle and a distance of 40 meters after the last hurdle. The 8 hurdles between the first and the last hurdles are equally spaced. What is the distance between hurdles?

POSTER PROBLEM

What fraction of 14-karat gold is not gold?

MONDAY

On an 8-digit calculator, what is the greatest number that can be displayed that is a multiple of 10?

TUESDAY

The story of *Cinderella* has been filmed more than any other story. The first film was made in 1898. The number of films since 1898 is 2 less than 5 dozen. How many films of *Cinderella* have been made?

WEDNESDAY

Francis Scott Key wrote the "Star Spangled Banner" in 1814. More than a century later it was designated the U.S. National Anthem. In what year did the "Star Spangled Banner" become the U.S. National Anthem? The sum of the digits of the year is 14. The tens' digit is greater than the ones' digit. The product of the digits is greater than zero.

THURSDAY

In cricket the pitch travels 22 yards and in baseball 60 feet 6 inches. How many inches longer is the cricket pitch?

FRIDAY

Construction of the Great Wall of China began in 246 B.C. and was completed 6 years more than 3 decades later. In what year was the Great Wall completed?

POSTER PROBLEM

How much heavier is a cube of iron measuring 3 feet on an edge than the same size cube of redwood?

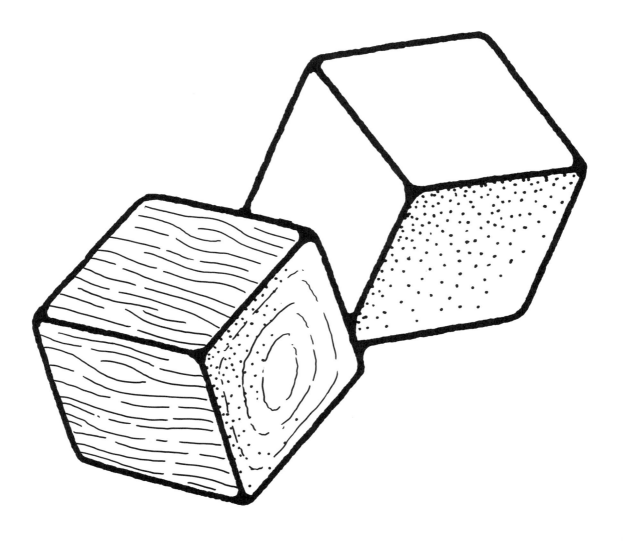

MONDAY

On December 17, 1903, Orville Wright made the first airplane flight at Kitty Hawk, North Carolina. Orville flew 120 feet in $\frac{1}{5}$ of a minute. On the average, how many feet did Orville fly each second?

TUESDAY

On the radio game show, "Take It or Leave It," contestants answer a maximum of 7 questions. For a correct answer to the first question, the contestant wins $1. After that, each question is worth twice as much as the previous question. If a contestant answers all 7 questions correctly, how much does the contestant win?

WEDNESDAY

Pennsylvania became a state before the first presidential election. In what year did Pennsylvania become a state? The tens' digit of the year is one more than the hundreds' digit and the ones' digit.

THURSDAY

In hockey, the width of the goal is 24 times the diameter of the puck. The diameter of the puck is the smallest odd prime number. How many feet wide is the goal?

FRIDAY

What is the sum of all the numbered cards in a regular deck of 52 playing cards?

POSTER PROBLEM

Nolan Ryan holds the record for the fastest pitch in baseball. He pitched a ball at a speed of 100.9 miles per hour. How many seconds did it take Ryan's pitch to travel from the pitcher's mound to home plate?

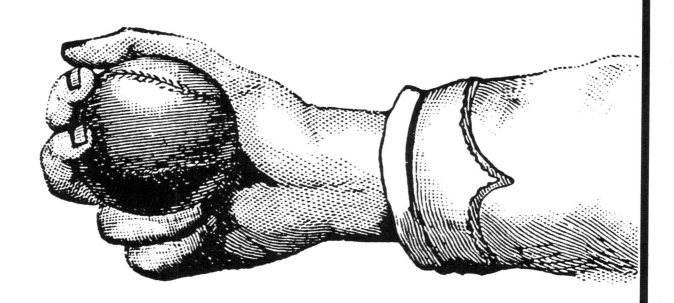

MONDAY

A person weighs 0.5 percent less at the Equator than at the Poles, due to the gravitational pull of Earth's mass on the mass of the human body. How much would someone weigh at the Equator if the person weighed 162 pounds at the North Pole?

TUESDAY

The shark used in the movie *Jaws* weighed 12 tons. A real shark may weigh as much as 112,000 pounds more than the movie shark. How many tons may a real shark weigh?

WEDNESDAY

The incandescent light and the diesel engine were both invented in years that contain the digits 1, 7, 8, and 9. The diesel engine was invented 18 years after the incandescent light. When was the light invented?

THURSDAY

In 1976 there were three times as many sports in the summer Olympics as in the winter Olympics. There were 14 more summer Olympic sports than winter Olympic sports. How many sports were in the Winter Olympics?

FRIDAY

How old was James Garfield when he became the 20th President of the United States? His age was the square of a prime number.

U. S. Secretary of State William H. Seward bought Alaska from Russia in 1867 for $7,200,000. To the nearest cent, how much was that per acre?

MONDAY

At sea level water boils at 212° Fahrenheit. At the top of Mt. Everest, 29,002 feet high, water boils at 159.8° Fahrenheit. How many degrees does the boiling point drop for every mile up from sea level to the top of Mt. Everest?

TUESDAY

The longest loaf of bread on record was 1,256 feet 2 inches long. If this bread had been cut into $\frac{1}{2}$ inch slices, how many slices of bread would there have been?

WEDNESDAY

Columbus Day commemorates Columbus's landing in America. The first Columbus Day celebration took place three centuries after Columbus landed in the Americas. When was the first Columbus Day celebration?

THURSDAY

The record time for swimming the English Channel is 4 hours and 20 minutes less than half a day. What is the record time?

FRIDAY

If a stack of 10 one-dollar bills is one millimeter high, how much money is in a stack of one-dollar bills one meter high?

POSTER PROBLEM

The horizontal length of the United States flag is called the FLY. The vertical width is called the HOIST. The UNION is the upper-left portion of the flag that shows the 50 stars on a blue background. What is the area of the UNION on a U.S. flag with a FLY of $9\frac{1}{2}$ feet and a HOIST of 5 feet?

Solution Key

Note: Students' solutions may differ from some of the solutions shown below, depending on which sources the students use.

Page 1

M	9999
Tu	$340
W	2 A.M.
Th	8100 square feet
F	624 foot bones

Page 2

10,000 pounds is 5 tons. One machine would harvest 25 tons in 5 days. Three machines would harvest 75 tons in 5 days.

Page 3

M	9 years
Tu	4 quarter notes
W	69 B.C.
Th	7 events
F	28 years

Page 4

June 6

Page 5

M	3 orbits
Tu	May, 1939
W	1824
Th	160 Ping-Pong balls
F	1974

Page 6

Sample answer using 26 inches as an average step. The highway distance between Los Angeles and San Francisco is 403 miles or 25,534,080 inches. You would need to take 982,080 steps to make the trip from Los Angeles to San Francisco.

Page 7

M	87 years
Tu	4 Academy Awards
W	13 years
Th	35 inches
F	360 baseballs

Page 8

There are 16 odd-number dates in months with 31 days. There are 15 odd-number dates in months with 30 days. There are 14 odd-number dates in February. There are 186 odd-number dates in a non-leap year.

Page 9

M	4,200 feet
Tu	4 squares
W	64 years
Th	5 rings
F	88 days

Page 10

The population of the U.S. in 1984 was about 235.1 million. There were about 156.7 million people wearing eyeglasses.

Page 11

M	3720 feet
Tu	February 3,1982
W	37 stars
Th	0 times
F	7 holes

Page 12

There are 898 steps in the Washington Monument. At the rate of 2 steps per second, it will take 7 minutes and 29 seconds to walk down.

Page 13

M	26
Tu	11,792 pounds
W	39 years old
Th	4 tennis balls
F	2076

Page 14

Answers may vary as an official NFL football is between $10\frac{7}{8}$ and $11\frac{7}{16}$ inches long. This sample answer uses 11 inches for the length of the football. A football field is 100 yards from goal line to goal line. It would take 328 11-inch footballs to reach from one goal line to the other.

Page 15

M	3 computers
Tu	1685
W	1951
Th	$^4/_{10}$ ($^2/_5$)
F	8 feet 2 inches

Page 16

The Gold Rush was 20 minutes longer than The Kid.

Page 17

M	981
Tu	1965
W	9 justices
Th	38 laps
F	4 square inches

Page 18

1 trillion, 380 billion pounds

Page 19

M	40 bee hummingbirds
Tu	$^5/_8$
W	1927
Th	44 ounces
F	36 notes

Page 20

The marathon is about 26 miles long. At the slower speed, it will take a runner 13 minutes longer to run the marathon.

Page 21

M	5 corners
Tu	1600 hours 44 minutes
W	February 12
Th	19 games
F	1935

Page 22

36 handshakes

Page 23

M	9:30 P.M.
Tu	1949
W	West Berlin, 2927 more people per square mile
Th	22 Series
F	48 minutes 55 seconds

Page 24

1 birthday

Page 25

M	6 feet
Tu	$34,810.13 per room
W	228 years
Th	60 feet
F	27.4 years

Page 26

Answers may vary as the distance to the moon is between 221,463 and 252,710 miles. For the sample answer the distance used is 240,000 miles. At 55 miles per hour, the trip would take 181.82 days. Since 1990 is a leap year, you would arrive on the moon on June 30, 1990.

Page 27

M	50 teeth
Tu	20 strings
W	1883
Th	3 feet
F	November 10, 1969

Page 28

A checkerboard is a square that has 8 rows of small squares with 8 squares in each row. There are 64 squares, each 1½ inches on a side.

Page 29

M	1 minute 30 seconds
Tu	170 singles
W	4 percent
Th	10 games
F	1790

Page 30

For the sample answer the tennis shoes weigh 1 pound 2 ounces and cost $24.99. The tennis shoes cost $22.21 per pound. A 4-door 1985 Chevrolet Caprice weighs 2,594 pounds and sells for about $14,310. The Chevrolet costs $5.52 per pound. The tennis shoes cost $16.69 per pound more than the car.

Page 31

M	C
Tu	49 squares
W	1950
Th	2 chukkers
F	1928

Page **32**

There are 33 floors or 396 feet. At 20 feet per second, the elevator would take about 20 seconds to travel from the 69th floor to the 102nd floor.

Page **33**

M	44° Fahrenheit
Tu	5 piano concertos
W	8 times
Th	200 laps
F	150 pounds

Page **34**

A regular set of dominoes contains 28 dominoes. The dominoes include the six doubles (0-0, 1-1, 2-2, 3-3, 4-4, 5-5, and 6-6) and all of the combinations of the numbers 0 through 6 in which no combination contains the same numbers. There are a total of 168 dots.

Page **35**

M	9 hours 50 minutes
Tu	1887
W	4 states
Th	140 feet
F	1929 (in France)

Page **36**

The road distance from San Francisco to New York is 3,036 miles. At 42 miles per hour, the car will take 72.3 hours. The air distance from San Francisco to New York is 2,571 miles. At 500 miles per hour the DC10 will take 5.1 hours. The car will take 67.2 hours longer than the DC10 to make the trip.

Page **37**

M	19.9 percent
Tu	$76.7 million
W	52.8 seconds
Th	9 markers
F	11.9 weeks

Page **38**

A metric ton is 1 million grams. A nickel is 5 grams. There are 3,200,000 nickels with a value of $160,000.

Page **39**

M	1/8 of iceberg
Tu	354 holes
W	14.7 percent
Th	100 points
F	98 yards

Page **40**

An earthquake measuring 2 on the Richter Scale is 10 times stronger than an earthquake measuring 1; an earthquake measuring 3 is 100 times stronger than an earthquake measuring 1. An earthquake measuring 8 is 10,000,000 times stronger than an earthquake measuring 1 and 1,000,000 times stronger than an earthquake measuring 2.

Page **41**

M	90°
Tu	48 hands
W	4 rows
Th	99 yards
F	.144 inches

Page **42**

The source of the Mississippi River is Itasca. The mouth of the River is the Gulf of Mexico. The length of the River is 2348 miles. At 3 miles per hour, it will take the toy boat 32 days 14 hours 40 minutes to reach the Gulf of Mexico.

Page **43**

M	169 fortnights
Tu	1883
W	39 Representatives
Th	400 square feet
F	45

Page **44**

September 28, 1887

Page **45**

M	$1.92
Tu	1896
W	361 people per square mile
Th	5 times
F	1852

Page **46**

A dollar bill is 15.7 centimeters or 6.18 inches. It will take 10,253 dollar bills to form a line one mile long.

Page **47**

M	Feburary 20, 1962
Tu	5 pipes
W	152 feet
Th	9 football fields
F	7 ounces

Page **48**

A "1" is displayed in naming the hours from 1 to 2, 10 to 11, 11 to 12, and 12 to 1; a total of 240 minutes. In each of the other hours, a "1" is displayed in the minutes for 01, 10, 11, 12, 13, 14, 15, 16, 17, 18, 19, 21, 31, 41, 51, or 15 minutes per hour for a total of 120 minutes in 8 hours. The "1" is displayed for a total of 360 minutes. A "9" is displayed to name the hour from 9 to 10. In each of the other 11 hours it is displayed in the minutes for 09, 19, 29, 39, 49, and 59, or 6 minutes per hour. A "9" is displayed for a total of 126 minutes. A "1" is displayed for 234 more minutes than a "9."

Page **49**

M	7.7 ounces
Tu	12 issues
W	January 1, 2200
Th	14 miles per hour
F	139.75 inches

Page **50**

The length of a tennis court is 78 feet. The diameter of a tennis ball is 2.5 inches and its circumference is 7.87 inches. The tennis ball would turn about 120 times.

Page **51**

M	CDXLIV
Tu	21 dots
W	1 daughter
Th	714 homeruns
F	15 years old

Page **52**

The *Mayflower* set sail on September 16 and landed on Cape Cod on November 19. (There is some question as to exactly when the *Mayflower* reached Cape Cod, but sometime between November 9 and 19.) The *QE2* takes 5 days to cross the Atlantic. The *QE2* would wait 59 days for the *Mayflower* to arrive.

Page **53**

M	1774
Tu	16 white keys
W	16 years
Th	12 pounds
F	1880

Page **54**

A cord is 4 feet high, 8 feet long, and 4 feet wide. Three hundred twenty cubic feet of wood is 2½ cords.

Page **55**

M	$130.00
Tu	1 Academy Award
W	1908
Th	12 medals
F	the eight ball

Page **56**

9 of spades, 7 of spades, 6 of clubs, 8 of diamonds, 2 of hearts

Page **57**

M	99
Tu	50.2 million
W	173 feet
Th	120 feet
F	2 cups

Page **58**

A sugar cube measures 1 centimeter on each edge. The large cube will measure 100 centimeters or 1 meter on a side.

Page 59

M	4 bills
Tu	364 (Getting the answer involves making a well-known triangular number pattern, Day 1=1, Day 2=1+2, Day 3=1+2+3, and so on. Then the totals for all the days are added together.)
W	7.1 days
Th	20 touchdowns
F	1951

Page 60

Japan

Page 61

M	1,000 stone
Tu	1756
W	1881
Th	$^{13}/_{18}$
F	7 terms

Page 62

Answers will vary. The population used here is 235,100,000 and the diameter of a penny as ¾ inch. The line of pennies would be about 2783 miles long.

Page 63

M	20 quire
Tu	14.3 percent
W	2 states
Th	9 feet
F	35 meters

Page 64

24-karat gold is $^{24}/_{24}$ or 100 percent gold. 14-karat gold is $^{14}/_{24}$ ($^{7}/_{12}$) gold; $^{10}/_{24}$ ($^{5}/_{12}$) is not gold.

Page 65

M	99,999,990
Tu	58 films
W	1931
Th	66 inches
F	210 B.C.

Page 66

Iron weighs 490 pounds per cubic foot. Redwood weighs 27 pounds per cubic foot. A cube of iron measuring 3 feet on an edge (27 cubic feet) weighs 13,230 pounds. The same size cube of redwood weighs 729 pounds. The cube of iron weighs 12,501 pounds more than the cube of redwood.

Page 67

M	10 feet per second
Tu	$127
W	1787
Th	6 feet
F	216

Page 68

The distance from the pitcher's mound to home plate is 60 feet 6 inches. Ryan's pitch took 0.4 of a second.

Page 69

M	161 pounds 3 ounces
Tu	68 tons
W	1879
Th	7 sports
F	49 years

Page 70

The area of Alaska is 586,412 square miles. There are 640 acres in a square mile. There are 375,303,680 acres in Alaska. Seward paid about 2 cents per acre.

Page 71

M	9.5° for each mile
Tu	30,148
W	1792
Th	7 hours 40 minutes
F	$10,000

Page 72

The UNION is $^{4}/_{10}$ of the FLY or $^{38}/_{10}$ feet. The UNION is $^{7}/_{13}$ of the HOIST or $^{35}/_{13}$ feet. The area of the UNION is 10 $^{3}/_{13}$ square feet.